A Consumer's Journey to Mental Health Recovery

By Beverly A. Johnson

AuthorHouse™
1663 Liberty Drive
Bloomington, IN 47403
www.authorhouse.com
Phone: 1-800-839-8640

Published by AuthorHouse   07/31/2012

ISBN: 978-1-4685-5654-4 (sc)
ISBN: 978-1-4685-5653-7 (e)

Library of Congress Control Number: 2012903509

CONTENTS

A Consumer's Journey to Mental Health and Recovery
is dedicated to my parents, the late Gloria and Leroy Johnson.

Preface

I was soul searching, and as a result I came up with these two booklets: Volume I, "Steps Toward Healthier and Happier Relationships," and Volume II, "Unraveling Inner Conflicts."

These breakthroughs led me to understand how people relate to each other on a daily basis. This helped me to learn some of the dynamics of human relationships in relation to my own experience.

The cowardly lion in "The Wizard of Oz" needed courage. And I needed the courage to write and publish the thoughts about my recovery. These two booklets will enlighten and inspire one to take charge of their rehabilitation towards their recovery.

Volume I

Steps Toward Healthier and Happier Relationships

SYNOPSIS

"Steps Toward Healthier and Happier Relationships" is about how I learned to connect with people in my daily life. This was essential for my recovery. By applying these examples one will be able to become more knowledgeable about how to improve their (human relations) people skills. The study consists of descriptions about predispositions, feelings and emotions, and group dynamics.

STEPS TOWARD HEALTHIER AND HAPPIER RELATIONSHIPS

My disability is paranoid schizophrenia, and I have been a consumer of psychiatric services since 1999. I believe that the paranoid part was devastating and debilitating. I was clearly psychotic. I was afraid of people and I never learned how to deal with them. Within the last three years, I finally became aware of how to deal with different behaviors in people. This is my story.

I will begin by telling you experiences that prompted me to write Steps Toward Healthier and Happier Relationships.

Going to LaGuardia Community College was the pivotal experience of my life. During that time, I was in my last semester at the college. I was having a lot of difficulties with the students in my class. I didn't know how to get along with other students. For example, when someone laughed, I thought they were laughing at me and I would begin to feel anxious. I was stressed for a long period of time and couldn't change my thinking. When someone made facial gestures, I perceived that as mocking me. This included facial gestures like raising the eyebrows, rubbing of the nose, and frowning. People in the class whispered or talked quietly to each other, and that left me suspicious that it was about me.

In terms of group dynamics, I was the in-between person. My emotions and communicating skills were not connected, and my predisposition was totally passive. In other words, I didn't know how to fend for myself. I decided to go to the dean of the college and ask if I could take independent courses. She said yes, but it turned out that I couldn't. I then returned to her office very emotional and crying. She then saw how serious the matter was, and called the director of counseling. I went with the director to his office and he began asking me questions. I told him that I was in therapy. He then asked for my therapist's name and when I was going to see her next. In a matter of a day or two, I was in session and the director called. After what seemed like hours, my therapist stated that I could not have independent classes. She also said that my professor knows about the situation and someone in his family has mental illness. In addition to going to my therapist, I also had to see a counselor at the college once a week. If those students had known that I was suffering from a mental disease, they would not have treated me like that. I was not trying to change people; I just wanted and still want respect. I made it through the final semester with flying colors.

It was trying to deal with situations like this that sparked me to write Steps Toward Healthier and Happier Relationships. During my school week as a student at The Howie the Harp Advocacy Center, studying to be a peer specialist, I began to have those past feelings creep up on me. Then it all came to me, and this is the result.

I finally learned how to relate to all kinds of people. To me, this is a systematic way of how I deal with dysfunctional people. It all started with my initial family.

My father was passive aggressive, and my mother was aggressive aggressive. I never learned how to deal with either of them, although my father was the lesser evil. I called my mother a "bully," and she was a bully for all it was worth. When I started middle school was when everything escalated. I was tormented, battered, and ridiculed by my classmates. I didn't know how to fend for myself, and knew it was wrong of them to do that to me. I was victimized all of my life by these kinds of people. Now that I knew how to label these types of people, I used that experience as a coping skill. For example, when one comes into contact with people who show us dysfunctional behavior, we have to work towards not being victimized. Therefore, we have to defuse, channel our feelings, and recognize that we all have the ability to overcome. In life there are a lot of adversities and injustices. No matter what hand of cards one is dealt in life, you can play those cards positively or negatively. It is up to the individual to persevere and make it in the world. Life is hot and cold, feast and famine, up and down. When happy things happen, one forgets about the bad things. When bad things happen, one forgets about the good things. There isn't really a happy medium.

There are three stages in the expression of anger:

Step1—The first is annoyance. You begin to feel your body respond mentally and physically.

Step2—The second is anger. The effect of stress is now apparent.

Step3—The third is rage, which at this point is out of control. This emotion is raw, unproductive, and you are liable to say or do anything. At this point, you don't have any fear.

It is important to be able to recognize and be in touch with your feelings and communicate. In other words, think before you respond. That's why you have to count to ten, over and over, to calm down. This is very difficult when you have never learned to do it.

In social or group dynamics, there is always going to be a facilitator in charge. This is an authority figure.

The group is made up of four components: the group's facilitators, the group leaders, the group's in-between people, and the group's followers.

Where does one lie among these four types?

1. Assertive—expressing one's rights without stepping on other's toes.

2. Aggressive, Aggressive—do not care about others nor their feelings. They are considered bullies.

3. Passive,Aggressive—people who internalize their feelings and do not communicate clearly or consistently. In other words, they hold themselves back. They retaliate to get back and are sneaky. They are also changeable, and can be passive or aggressive.

4. Passive—these people don't have any reaction. They go along with whatever or whomever.

When we figure out which of the above listed predispositions we are, this is the first step in the process of dealing with our difficulties.

There are two levels of reactions: verbal and physical. Verbal means that you get an actual response. Whether it is harsh, loud, monotone, or silent, one reacts and needs to respond with some sort of plan of action. Physical means that one is assaulted, and bodily harm has been done. Some verbal reactions involve facial gestures or body language. A raise of the eyebrows, rubbing of the nose, a grimaced face could possibly state that one is unapproachable. Body language can mean waving hands and other body movements. There is also a response that's subtle, almost invisible, which could mean anything to the reaction of one's feelings.

This is my way of dealing with people who are assertive, aggressive aggressive, passive aggressive, and passive. It helps me to be in touch with my emotions of annoyance, anger, rage, and try to think before I respond. I use it to understand where I like to be in terms of group dynamics. I really don't want to deal with someone who is aggressive aggressive; and I don't have the disposition to fight back to get my needs met. I have to go around the difficulties of these people to assert myself. These people somehow believe that they can disrespect others, due to their own dysfunction and unfortunateness.

I won't have many disagreements with people that are assertive because they know that there is enough for everyone, and we're all in this together.

In terms of group dynamics, these people are the true leaders.

If I meet aggressive aggressive people in any given circumstances, I don't go into fight or flight. Instead, I will approach the situation the second time around with the knowledge that these people don't know any better. They are trying to challenge me to see if I can deal with or handle their behavior. I know I will sink before I can swim. This is a procedure that works about 99 ½% of the time. It is the only way I see fit to survive. Whether it's a group of people or individuals, I just say "good morning" or whatever time of day it is. Yes, I can say things like "how are you doing?", "what's going on?", "what did you do on the weekend?" etc. These responses are all on the surface, and that is all one needs to do to get through. In terms of group dynamics, they try to be the leaders but it is apparent that they don't have the necessary tools. Their personality becomes apparent, and they are exposed for who they really are.

Now for passive aggressive people. These people are private in terms of their feelings or communications. In other words, these people don't show any emotion. They look for any chance to get even. At least aggressive aggressive people let you know right away. Again, I will use the same approach and that really does work. One is aware of these people and understands their behavior. It's like a sweet and bitter scenario. In terms of group dynamics, they are middle people.

Now, for passive people. These people are afraid and they comply with everything. They just don't make waves. They just exist. It's sad that these people can't really fend for themselves. When I see these people, I want to help them in every way. They are often used by people who don't care about them. In terms of group dynamics, they are the followers.

The process is the mirror of affirmation I get from these people, and I feel good when they begin to respond back to me. My purpose is to help people and try to give back what I have received.

I also want to protect myself and not end up the victim, saying "woe's me and I can't deal with those people". No one can read your mind, so you must express your feelings and communicate. We need to understand where we are in terms of how to express our anger; the position we are at in group dynamics; and how we deal with assertive people, aggressive aggressive people, passive aggressive people, and passive people. There is really no easy way out but by beginning to understand one's self through this process. It is never too late to change and grow.

Steps Toward Healthier and Happier Relationships and How to Apply Them:

The predisposition one would want to develop is assertive.

In terms of group dynamics, one would like to eventually be one of the leaders.

In terms of expressing one's emotions and communicating, we should be able to recognize their feelings and state what they are early on.

This practice can be used in all interpersonal relationships

Therefore, assertive people observe and become aware of predispositions, e.g., assertive, aggressive aggressive, passive aggressive, and passive.

Assertive people then realize what each of these people's needs are and what they have to give.

Assertive

I like being around these people because I find them to be helpful and sensitive. I like assertive people because they are direct, frank, and honest. They don't give mixed messages and are straightforward. These people are conscientious and find people enjoyable. I try to emulate these people and direct my energies in the same manner as they do. I realize that it doesn't hurt me to be positive and help people, even if they can't help me back. It really feels good to try to help people and make a difference in others' lives. Now, my relationships have definitely improved since I learned to be assertive. I find myself growing every day.

Assertive Example

When I first started working at one of the major department stores, my job was to sell women's shoes. My boss was very considerate and direct with me. One day, a customer wanted a pair of shoes that didn't come in a wide width. I tried to explain to the customer that this brand of shoes only came in medium widths. I asked if I could show her a similar pair. The customer then said that I didn't want to be of help, and why didn't I go back to check? Next, she started yelling "Where is the manager?" I went and got the boss, who was in his office. When I told him what was going on, he came out on the floor. Before he came out front, he told me that I did the right thing and not to beat myself up over it. He explained to the customer that the shoes didn't come in wide widths. Also, the boss told the customer that I was a good worker. The customer then decided to try on the similar style shoes.

This was a good experience with someone who is assertive, and it was a wonderful experience to work with him.

Aggressive Aggressive

Aggressive aggressive people are just the opposite of assertive people. As a child and adult, I always retreated from aggressive people and their behaviors frightened me. When I presented myself in a scared way, they picked up on this. I just didn't know how to defend myself when I had to deal with these people. Often, I was afraid of these people and allowed them to verbally and sometimes physically abuse me. I didn't question the aggressive aggressive people's behaviors or ask myself "Why is this happening to me?" Aggressive aggressive people are self-centered and want to control others. As an adult, I learned how to deal with these people through understanding their behaviors. When they present themselves to me by acting like bullies, being cocky and fearless, I now don't allow them to disrespect me.

I have changed my outlook and stand up for my rights. Now I have better relationships with these people. I don't let them enter my space and allow them to treat me any way they feel like. I want respect from these aggressive aggressive people.

Aggressive Aggressive Example

I went to the local cleaners where there is a very aggressive aggressive owner. I was hoping that this person wasn't working at this time, since I would have liked to avoid him. Yes, I could have gone somewhere else, but this cleaners is convenient. There was no doubt that the work they did was outstanding. Whatever I brought to be cleaned and pressed was to my liking.

Every time that I went to the local cleaners, the owner knew how to get me. It seems that the owner wanted to perpetuate the situation when he showed his aggressive aggressive behavior. I wouldn't retaliate back when this happened, and I usually withdrew. I didn't have the ability to stop this pattern of fleeing. I finally realized to react to the owner in a lighter, more on the surface manner.

One day, as I proceeded to go into the store, this person was there. He stated harshly and loudly "How many items do you have?" I then proceeded to say something, then realized and told myself "Wait a minute. Am I going to allow this behavior towards me again?" I knew that I didn't want to perpetuate this further, so I said

"How are you doing?" The reply was "all right", and instantly there was a change of behavior. Ever since, the owner now is very cordial and polite to me.

Passive Aggressive

Passive aggressive people are back stabbers. When I dealt with these people in the past, I really thought that they were my friends. I trusted them only to find out that they are not nice people at all. I had thought that they were on my side, and sometimes I revealed things about myself only to be deceived by them. These people appear to be two-faced, but actually they have a hard time getting in touch with their angry feelings. Instead, they unconsciously detour these feelings and make the other person they are angry at, angry for them.

These people really have to be studied for a while because it's hard to know where they're coming from. Unlike aggressive aggressive people who are more up front with expressing their true selves, passive aggressive people do not reveal their true selves right away. Although it still takes time to be aware of these people, I am now better able to understand them and not let them fool me.

Passive Aggressive Example

I had a friend for a few years who was always happy to accept a ride to Brooklyn, from Manhattan club meetings. She didn't like driving her own car because she was afraid of Manhattan traffic.

When my boyfriend had the car, I would ask her to take me somewhere local. Her reply was often, "I am busy and maybe I could take you another time." When I told her about how my boyfriend and I always took her to meetings and back, she said "Sorry I was so much trouble."

Two weeks went by, and I called her to ask for a ride. She said, "Sure, I can drive you." I waited an hour, then called, and her line was busy. She never showed up nor bothered to call. At this point, I felt used, and no longer could ask her for help.

Also, this friend had always called me at late hours to talk about her relationship issues and problems. Even if I was out, she would leave desperate-sounding messages. This was the turning point of our "so-called" relationship. I found out from another friend that she said that I'm a lousy driver and that my boyfriend never lets me drive alone. This was not true. I started crying and was annoyed at this false accusation.

I then realized that she wasn't a true friend, but decided to give her another chance. This woman and I hadn't talked as much on the phone as before. Then, one Sunday, she called at 8 a.m. and woke my light-sleeper boyfriend. Instead of asking for me or leaving a message, she kept talking to him about her ill sister. She found out that he had had less than four hours of sleep due to airport delays. Later, I left a message to please not to call so early on a Sunday. Instead of calling to apologize, she just ignored my message. After about one month, I unexpectedly bumped into the woman at a different meeting. I started to say "Hello", when she rudely cursed me out and walked away!

I felt badly about losing what I had considered a friend, even after giving her a second chance. This person is definitely passive aggressive.

Passive

I have seldom come across many passive people in my life. If anything, I want to help these people in any way that I can. I don't see them as a threat, but people who are very quiet and greatly afraid to make waves.

Passive people are overlooked because of their quietness and shy natures.

Passive Example

I have a childhood friend who is very afraid and terribly shy. She just about goes along with anything others do. I try to help her by saying "why don't you speak your mind?" "You know that you don't like this or want that." She would always reply "I just don't want to make waves, so I go along with everyone else." I always tell her that what you think or do is your perfect right. "Therefore, why don't you just speak your mind and assert yourself?"

Finally, she shared something with me about her life and how she became passive. This is her story. Growing up in a household of nine children, she was born somewhere in the middle. She wasn't the oldest who got all of the attention, and, basically had to watch over the younger children. Also, she wasn't the baby whom everyone adored. Her parents didn't have time for her, so she spent a lot of time by herself. She was used to being lost in a group and going along with what the adults asked. Later, during her career as a Reference Librarian, she encountered a director who wasn't good at managing the staff. The director totally leaned on my friend and it became a necessity to break out of her passiveness. The staff needed a manager/leader.

Finally, my friend realized that she had to say how she truly felt! From now on, she told me "I will stand up for myself and be assertive instead of passive."

To sum up, these steps toward achieving healthier and happier relationships have helped me immensely.

I hope you will find them a practical tool for taking control of your own relationships with people.

Volume II

Unraveling Inner Conflicts

SYNOPSIS

"Unraveling Inner Conflicts" is about my struggles (which are within) to come to terms with my mental illness. I came up with a theory by observing myself and the world at large, and by coming up with a strategy for my recovery. Inner conflicts are automatic, unconscious thoughts, habits, and rituals which one uses in order to shield themselves from their trauma. We all have inner conflicts.

UNRAVELING INNER CONFLICTS

Why do I automatically think people don't like me? Why do I automatically think that people want to make fun of me? Why do I automatically think that people want to harm me? This is my belief system. This is how I survived.

It all started when I was working in a department store. I worked there for a few years full-time. Towards the latter part of the third year I found myself in my room lying in bed not able to move. I couldn't eat nor drink. I didn't even get up to use the bathroom or shower.

The next thing I knew I was on an AMTRAK train heading toward Washington D.C. to see my older brother. I was accompanied by my half-sister and younger brother.

Once there my older brother, his girlfriend, and her sister didn't question me, but just watched me as my episodes went on. I would look out the window facing the backyard and see a garbage pail. I yelled down to a woman to move the pail so if I was going to jump I wouldn't land up in the garbage. That failed because she didn't listen.

Then I ravaged my half-sister's pocketbook and found a bottle of pills. I just looked at them like it was candy and spilled the pills onto the bed and left them there. I don't think I was trying to take my life. I was just carrying on and not making any kind of sense because I wasn't myself. All those strange things I did nobody saw me doing.

Still I barely ate or drank anything. My older brother was having a party and fashion show, and I went to it. Toward the end of the event I went over to the DJ and told him to stop the freaking music, and he just ignored me.

Back at the apartment my head hit the pillow and I was out like a light. Then the next morning my older brother drove me from Washington D.C. to a hospital in Brooklyn, New York. When I arrived my whole family was there. The doctor told my mother that if she didn't hospitalize me he would do so anyway and so she agreed.

Once up on the ward the nurse gave me a peanut butter and jelly sandwich and a cup of something that tasted like pineapple juice. When the lights went out I got up to go to the bathroom, but before I was able to make the trip down the hall, I threw up whatever that cocktail was and told the nurse I did. This was the start of having to take medication for the rest of my life.

Morning arrived and I got up to have breakfast of which I hardly ate anything. My family members came to visit me in the afternoon, and then all of a sudden my tongue went to the back of my mouth. A patient ran and got the nurse. She gave me something to drink and that did the trick to stop me from choking on my tongue.

In arts and crafts I made a doll and later gave it to my mother. I started feeling better so when I saw the doctor known as the psychiatrist I asked him if I could go home and he said "yes". My mother was supposed to pick me up but I left before she got there. I caught the bus home and came into the house.

I wasn't out of the hospital even a week when my half-sister came into my room saying something about playing music and started fighting with me. I fought back and the next thing I knew the police were in the house. They took me back to the hospital and I stayed there one night.

At this point I knew I needed somewhere else to live. My best friend in the world asked me if I wanted to live with her. I said yes I will be your roommate. So reluctantly, with tears because I was apprehensive, I took all of my stuff and moved out without looking back.

When I returned to the hospital I was given medicine, the name of my therapist, and where the office was located. My mother came with me for that first visit and she talked to the therapist while I waited in the hallway. The next visit I was told that my mother wasn't going to be a part of my therapy, and that I had a major breakdown. In 1982 I was diagnosed with Paranoid Schizophrenia. What did that mean? I didn't know. Did this scare me? No.

Then the therapist took me to see the psychiatrist. At times I was given too much medicine, sometimes very little medicine, and other times none at all. I knew to come back so they adjusted the medicine to just the right dosage. I didn't have a problem taking the medicine and that made me compliant. Every time I went to the psychiatrist my therapist came with me.

The side effects were minimal: dry mouth, which subsided, and weight gain that was a problem, but I was able to control it. I took the meds at night but in the morning it was hard to wake up.

Even though I took the meds I began hearing voices and it startled me to the point that I would turn around a lot to see if anybody was around me, and no one ever was. I learned that the voices were coming from me, and that nobody could hear them but me. Even with the medications I heard voices. The voices would come randomly. It was a woman's voice. It taunted me a lot, but I finally was able not to let the voices affect me. They eventually subsided and to this day I no longer am bothered by them. The voices went away before the paranoia did.

The paranoia was the worst of it for sure. I was afraid and suspicious of most people who I thought might hurt me.

I went through a serious ordeal with this and didn't expect to see light at the end of the tunnel. On the other hand, I didn't think I was doomed either. As I muddled my way through the trials and tribulations of the illness, suddenly the words "inner conflicts" dawned on me. So what do inner conflicts mean and how do they apply to me?

For starters, I recognize that the struggle was within me. It was difficult enough dealing with external conflicts, but it was worse coping with my inner conflicts without realizing where they came from. The worst are the inner conflicts because it is like one never realizes that it is coming from them.

I think my childhood traumas started when I was three years old. This is the first episode I remembered. My half-sister saw me with matches by the window, and kept yelling and yelling. She went above and beyond instead of telling me don't play with matches. This continued until my parents came home. My mother beat me and yelled mean words at me. I was unable to talk to them or ask any questions. This is when they broke my spirits and made me afraid of them.

Through the years people asked me why I fret and frown all the time. I just didn't learn or know how to smile.

Today, physically and verbally attacking children is considered child abuse, and these abuses brought on my mental illness. Those events interfered with some of my brain's development and my ability to learn.

Inner conflicts are emotional disturbances that may torment individuals throughout their lifetime. The severity of the inner conflicts is sometimes rather difficult for the person to come to terms with. The struggle is within the person them self. We all have inner conflicts to one degree or the other.

This is how I learned to deal with my inner conflicts. I hated when my mode entered into either flight or fight. When a child is beaten down it is either going to be aggressive or timid with people. However, it's the timid child who gets the help because people are more willing to approach him or her.

From nature I had a susceptibility to be sensitive. I couldn't interpret the distortions of my perceptions. Virtually throughout my life I could never make sense out of my family's responses to me.

My parent's behavior was aggressive. Therefore, some people who reminded me of my parent's aggressive behavior would trigger the same anxiety that would make me scared of them as well.

I began to be aware of my own behavior and other people's response to it. I thought of coping skills to counteract my feelings and thinking. I would recite to myself, "The observation (observing myself) of awareness (realizing my behavior) through coping skills (remembering what to say to myself to keep it healthy), through maintaining (staying on target and knowing the triggers) with maintenance (even if I get a set-back the goal is to constantly work at it). Therefore, I would clarify my thoughts that everything is a distortion until you get a direct response, whether verbal or physical. Is this really happening? Is this really going on (reality check)? This helped clarify whether my thoughts were based on the reality of events that were happening. Then I told myself that "there is nothing to fear but fear itself."

So when thoughts automatically came into mind that people don't like me, people wanted to make fun of me, and people possibly wanted to harm me, then I would recite these truths over and over to myself. These thoughts of what is and what isn't reality started to become less bothersome. Learning how not to react to old time thinking, and dismissing paranoid thoughts can only make one free from the thought patterns one had to use to survive.

However, if you have mental illness it becomes more difficult making a decision. Then it becomes a real struggle and challenge.

To sum up, the inner conflicts one is subjected to are very real. Resolving one's conflicts with self-knowledge is no little feat but it can be done. Now, one can become less traumatized and be a true advocate for one's self in their recovery.

Volume III

The Nature
and Nurture of
Personalities

Topic: The way one learns has a direct effect on how the brain functions and can determine an individual's choices in his or her life's vocations.

Thesis: Both nature and nurture affect how we think and learn.

Sources Used: Personal observations

Conclusion: What one is given from nature can be enhanced or blocked by the interventions of nurture.

THESIS

The mind is to some extent both known and unknown. However, the brain and its complexities determine one's future outcome.

I find myself connected when I allow it. Stresses of the environment, and the injustices and adversities which are out of my control cause the change in how I feel. There is no way to have my feelings flow and constantly stay steady if I don't set my mind to it.

TOPIC

How we think, feel, and perceive the world around us can result in disorders. How does one remove these toxic events from the realms of one's life? Why can't the immune system just reject certain things that are harmful to our very good? Our psyches travel to many extremes which can be either lows or highs.

SOURCES USED

I have examined myself and realize we are not the same. Doesn't this explain individualism? Why do some people have better memories and more mature emotions that are necessary for learning? We are not all going to be cookie-cut outs!

Isn't it interesting how the mind can have a direct impact on individuals' lives? We expect a balance between mind and success. It is not easy to resolve this question, but is life unfair just because the mind malfunctions? I have come to think that there is always going to be someone smarter than you, someone prettier than you, and someone with more money than you. How does one with limitations obtain higher education which connects to all aspects in life, arts, sports, leadership, and other vocations? It is a misconception to think that life is fair.

Not to be pessimistic, but these are all factors when looking for work, whether it be passion or not. Money has been shown to relate to having a better life. Yes, money is not the end all or be all, but we can live better lives with it. But then again, you have the question of a Dr. Jekyll and Mr. Hyde type of behavior, a response which can lead to difficulties in life. You can have this madness in you, but also have some normality in you. This is a challenge in all facets of life. Some people are more susceptible to mental illness, Autism, Down Syndrome, Asperger's, or any other disorder relating to brain malfunction. Is there a golden rule that explains all this? Yes! We have to accept what has been given to us, both nature and nurture. The qualities of our home life, including parental nurturing, play a major role in our development.

The conditions of your environment should include good medical, educational, and social experiences because we all need these in life, then we are mature enough to cope with life. In a larger framework, there are laws and information services in place to prevent and protect people against domestic abuse, child abuse, etc., but there is much more work to be done.

CONCLUSION

The components and elements of the brain play a clear role and house the constellation of personality traits. Distortions and extremes of personalities therefore reflect complex interactions between the elements and parts of the brain, our DNA, and our social experiences.

The science of mapping of the brain is important for us all because it will help us understand our uniqueness and the gifts that we bring to the world.

To sum up, there are many variables involving how our personalities are expressed, whatever one has been given, use it and feel good about it.

Volume IV

The Essentials of
Healthy Thinking

THE ESSENTIALS OF HEALTHY THINKING

I came up with a method that's being used to measure feelings and emotions, predispositions, and group dynamics. My study, "The Essentials of Healthy Thinking" was conducted to challenge and prove that group dynamics is universally needed to understand social behavior. I used a variety of people. The survey consisted of these three questions:

1. If I give you a trillion dollars or good mental health, which one would you take?
2. If I give you a trillion dollars or love which one would you take?

3. Which one of the following is necessary for life in general?

1. Feelings and Emotions – Feelings and emotions consist of being able to say these words when in stressful situations:
    a. "I'm annoyed" – You begin to feel your body respond mentally and physically.
    b. "I'm angry" – The effect of stress is now apparent.
    c. "I'm in rage" – This emotion is raw, out of control, and you are liable to say or do anything. At this point you don't have any fear.

2. Group Dynamics – In social or group dynamics, there is always going to be a facilitator in charge. This is an authority figure. The group is made up of four components: the group's facilitators, the group leaders, the group's in-between people, and the group's followers. Group Dynamics is about the placement of people in group settings. You have the facilitator in the group, and the people in the group:
    a. Leaders
    b. In-between people

c. The followers
3. Predispositions   - Last but not least, predisposition predicts/explains how people behave.
a. Assertive - Assertive people are direct, frank, and honest. They express their rights without stepping on other's toes. They don't give mixed messages and are straightforward. These people are conscientious and find people enjoyable.
b. Aggressive Aggressive - Aggressive aggressive people are just the opposite of assertive people. They do not care about others nor their feelings. They are considered bullies.
These people are self-centered and want to control others.
c. Passive Aggressive - Passive aggressive people are back stabbers. These people internalize their feelings and do not communicate clearly or consistently. They appear to be two-faced, but actually they have a hard time getting in touch with their angry feelings. Instead, they unconsciously detour these

feelings and make the other person they are angry at, angry for them.

d. Passive – These people don't have any reaction. These people are afraid and they comply with everything. They don't make waves.

The participants were only allowed to choose one answer. Overall most people chose feelings and emotions. However, when it came to predispositions, it was almost unanimously ignored. The majority of people in the study chose feelings and emotions. On many different levels most stated that the need to pick feelings and emotions was more eminent to living in the social world.

This experiment led me to believe the importance of how human emotions are necessary for human courtesy. However, group dynamics is the right answer of choice, which means "the dynamic processes, operations, and changes that occur within social groups, which affect patterns of communication, conflict, decision making, influence, and power", "The American Psychological Association (APA) dictionary of psychology".

As I was growing up, my feelings and emotions weren't connected. Socially I was passive. In group dynamics, I was the in-between person. What I mean in terms of feelings and emotions is how one deals with stressful events in life.

People in general first react by being annoyed, then angry, and finally enraged. The stressors come from the external environment. In terms of my anger, I didn't know how to express it. I have evolved through the years and my fate was better because I wasn't aggressive.

Predispositions are based on biological markings and expressed as behaviors one shows in their environments, which could be assertive, aggressive aggressive, passive aggressive, and passive. Although the goal is to be assertive, behaviors can fluctuate. My predisposition was passive, and that subjected me to other people's whims, which was emotionally destructive.

The last of the theory is group dynamics. Group dynamics started with evolution and the animals. Therefore, in humans the nuclear family is the first group. Why are groups formed? To show an assembly of people that may or may not believe in the same ideas, but to gain some sort of togetherness in a civilized fashion. I was the in-between person in group dynamics. I was a thinker, independent, curious, and a wonderer.

As a result of these findings from the survey I conducted, it proves that my booklet, "Steps Toward Happier and Healthier Relationships" logically follows my thinking about feelings and emotions, group dynamics, and predispositions. It was the group dynamics that taught me to become an independent thinker, and how I survived.

The formula consists of feelings and emotions which is a direct link to love (love of life, happy to be alive). Predisposition coincides with good mental health. Group dynamics is the sole unknown variable that doesn't connect with either, and that is the suitable choice. The role gives one a function in life. Once one knows what role they play in terms of group dynamics, then they can move toward different arenas in the other groups. Therefore, the right answer to this survey question is group dynamics.

The finding of the study makes me realize that my being the in-between person of the group explains my survival. The fact of the matter is that some of those surveyed answered group dynamics. The first two questions mostly everybody agreed upon without hesitation. Overall, the theory turned out to be inclusive, and as a result, beneficial to me and the world at large.

Volume V

A Therapist Who
Makes a Difference

A THERAPIST WHO MAKES A DIFFERENCE

Whether the therapist is in private practice or other settings for example, clinic or hospital it is imperative that intake be conducted by the therapist. This gives therapists better knowledge about what to ask them. This may be an enlightening experience without a doubt, but is necessary in order for the therapist to proceed.

It is not only vital to the success of the relationship with the therapist but that connection will most often set the pace if it is a good fit.

Therefore, therapy should be centered on a good fit between therapist and the person in need of help. Once the consumer has an emotional breakdown, the magnitude of the vulnerability of the consumer is critical. They don't know what is going on or what is happening to them. This can be very frightening or upsetting. There are issues which involve an array of circumstances. For instance the first hospital experience, diagnosis, medication, and the family dynamics etc. There is a difference in terms of the severities and extremes of the effects of mental illness, and usually at this point everything may be dysfunctional. This may cause the person to be very emotional or angry with aggression as a result.

A therapist should have humility, they should relate well, and they should show empathy. Having and showing mutual respect will go a long way. The job of a therapist is to help not only build up the consumer's strengths but to help them identify their weaknesses.

When a consumer makes a major breakthrough in their treatment, both therapist and consumer will feel gratified. At this point progress is made and everybody will feel it and know it.

Yes there are setbacks and that is where the challenges lie. When a mental health crisis arises this is where the therapists' skills are eminent, in terms of a matter of life and death or rehospitalization. This is all very real and does happen. The law states that if a person is a danger to oneself or others, then the penal system gets involved.

Therefore, the therapist should be prepared for these difficult times. It's apparent that the consumer's struggles are within themselves, but the support of a competent therapist will help them at such times.

This is a serious job for the therapist to undertake whether it is long term or short term. These sessions will be ongoing and the therapist should have the tenacity, endurance, and motivation in keeping up the momentum. Never forget that the therapists who are working with consumers that have mental illness are doing the best they can.

This is where the skillfulness of the therapist comes into play and how successful the treatment will be.

With the discretion of the therapist sometimes it may be necessary for the therapist to reach out and go above and beyond their traditional sessions. Some of the ways a therapist can make a consumer feel special is by becoming a surrogate. The American Heritage Dictionary's definition of the word surrogate is "One that takes the place of another: substitute." This is not an enabler. This may be the only connection the consumer has in terms of letting them know that someone does care. In addition, a therapist should keep in mind that this can make a world of a difference for a consumer who has mental illness.

There is no ideal consumer, however helping them towards greater sustainability and their rehabilitation will definitely lead the consumer to a more focused perspective towards their recovery.

Volume VI

Poems & Song

FEAR

Learning to deal with people is a dilly
What do you expect when you're a lilly
The surroundings are scary and frightening
To someone who's not used to lightening
What could a person like that do
When they are afraid to pursue

WHAT NEW HEAVENS

What new heavens have awakened in me
The clear blue vision of the sky is of a strange
blue
Could it be the bluest of the blues I see
My thoughts are strange today, and you
I say the clouds are what makes the sky
The clear vision of the sky is of a strange blue
Could it be the bluest of the blues, and why
The almighty eternal sky shall always surprise us
The power and the beauty of the sky we cannot
deny
A hasty departure to you, cumulonimbus
What new heavens have awakened in me
Could it be the bluest of the blues I see

WHAT NEW HEAVENS

What new heavens have awakened in me
Could it be the bluest of the blues I see
I say the clouds are what makes the sky for us to
see
My thoughts are strange today
How about you
The power and beauty of the sky we can't deny
Beauty of the sky we can't deny
I feel so wonderfully divine passing my time
in the sunshine
Hoping that tomorrow will be mine
What new heavens have awakened in me
My thoughts are changing so suddenly
Casting aside any hope and dreams
of inner peace
My thoughts are strange today
How about you

The power and the beauty of the sky we can't
deny

Beauty of the sky we can't deny
You come up in my dreams
all the time
What new heavens have awakened in me
Could it be the bluest of the blues I see
I say the clouds are what makes the sky
for us to see
What new heavens
What new heavens
Have awakened in me

Epilogue

The word dumb has many belittling meanings. We all know what the word smart means and how different it is looked upon when said. Being labeled dumb is not only caustic to the individual, but may lead to the individual giving up on learning.

People tend to label people who learn differently and don't take into consideration the effects it may have on that person. Keep in mind, everybody learns differently. The dunce hat always betrayed a child who couldn't learn, as he or she sat in a corner at the back of the classroom. If this is not humiliating, what is?

There are different styles of learning. Maybe one is a late bloomer? Unfortunately, in terms of work, one is paid according to how they learn and what they can do.

I always talk about how one can make money; for example, from being employed by private sector, non–profit, civil service, pastoral work, entrepreneur, getting a degree, do trades, and talent/entertainment.

Utilizing one's gifts in any of these arenas can be a challenge, but it can be done. Getting a head start by going to the library and doing research can be helpful. Ask the librarian for the "Occupational Outlook Handbook." Also, having your intellectual strengths and weaknesses evaluated by a professional is good strategy.

What can I tell you? There's always going to be somebody who's a janitor versus a doctor. Should one feel less valued? Of course not; you do the best you can. Any way one looks at this, one must strive to be the best he or she can be.

ABOUT THE AUTHOR

Beverly Johnson

A native New Yorker, she is still in recovery and sustaining her mental health. She has been an invited speaker at several major New York City hospitals and universities to lecture about her recovery.